THE ROAD TO SUSTAINABLE SUCCESS

NAVIGATING THE PATHWAY TO YOUR GOALS

KAILASHI PUNIT D.

Made with ♥ on the Notion Press Platform
www.notionpress.com

To all those who have inspired me to pursue my own definition of success, and to those who are on their own journey towards achieving their goals.

To my family, Papa , Mummy and Indu Didi who have supported and encouraged me every step of the way, and who have taught me the value of hard work and perseverance.

To my mentors and coaches, Professors and Administrative Officers I worked with and learned a lot about, Who have challenged me to grow and learn, and who have provided me with guidance and support throughout my career.

To my colleagues and friends, who have inspired me with their own achievements and who have shown me the power of building strong relationships and networks.

And to all the readers of this book, who are seeking to achieve their own version of success. May this book provide you with the insights, strategies, and inspiration you need to achieve your goals and make your dreams a reality?

This book is dedicated to you.

Contents

Foreword *vii*

Preface *ix*

Acknowledgements *xiii*

Prologue *xv*

Sustainable success *xvii*

1. The Success Mindset: Cultivating A Positive And Resilient Mindset For Success 1
2. Clarifying Your Vision: Crafting A Clear And Compelling Vision For Your Life And Career 8
3. Building Habits: Creating Habits And Routines That Support Your Success 12
4. Embracing Failure And Learning From Mistakes: How To Turn Setbacks And Failures Into Opportunities For Growth 16
5. Finding Mentors And Coaches: Building A Support System To Help You Achieve Your Goals 20
6. Overcoming Self-doubt And Imposter Syndrome: Strategies For Managing Self-doubt And Imposter Syndrome 24
7. The Power Of Networking: Building Relationships And Leveraging Your Network For Success 28
8. Leading With Emotional Intelligence: Developing Emotional Intelligence Skills For Effective Leadership 32

Contents

9. Time Management And Productivity: Maximizing Your Time And Productivity To Achieve Your Goals 37
10. Maintaining Work-life Balance: Balancing Your Personal And Professional Life To Avoid Burnout And Increase Happiness 42
11. How To Achieve Sustainable Success: Corporates 46
12. How To Achieve Sustainable Success: Individuals 50
About The Author 55
Summary 57
Important Points Covered 59
References 61
Further 63
Disclaimer 65

FOREWORD

I am honored to write the foreword for this book on achieving success. As someone who has achieved a level of success in my own life, I am always eager to share my experiences and insights with others who are seeking to achieve their own goals.

One of the things that I appreciate most about this book is the breadth of topics covered. From cultivating a success mindset to building supportive habits and relationships to maintaining work-life balance, this book offers a comprehensive guide to achieving success in all aspects of our lives.

But what I appreciate even more is the author's approach to these topics. Rather than offering a one-size-fits-all approach, the author recognizes that success means different things to different people. Instead, the author provides a framework for readers to identify their own definition of success and offers practical strategies and insights for achieving that vision.

Throughout this book, readers will find inspiring quotes from successful individuals who have achieved greatness in their respective fields. These quotes serve as a reminder that success is not an overnight achievement, but a journey that requires hard work, perseverance, and a willingness to learn and grow.

As someone who has had the privilege of working with successful individuals from various industries, I can attest to the value of the strategies and insights shared in this book. Whether you are a recent graduate starting your career or a seasoned professional seeking to take your business to the next level, the lessons in this book are applicable to all stages of life and career.

I commend the author for creating a resource that is both practical and inspiring. This book is not just a guide to achieving success, but a reminder that success is a journey and that we are all capable of achieving greatness with the right mindset, habits, and relationships.

I encourage readers to approach this book with an open mind and a willingness to learn and grow. Whether you are just starting out on your journey toward success or are looking for new strategies to take your career or personal life to the next level, this book has something to offer.

Congratulations to the author on creating a valuable resource for anyone seeking to achieve success in their life and career.

Sincerely,

Professor Dr. Indu Sharma
Editor

PREFACE

Success is not about achieving but its about maintaining what has already been achieved and always demands for Sustainability- Kailashi Punit D.

Success is a word that is often thrown around in our daily lives, but what does it truly mean? Is it wealth, power, or status? Is it a feeling of fulfillment and happiness? The truth is, success means something different to everyone, and it can be achieved in countless ways. However, there are certain principles and habits that successful people share, and these can be learned and applied to our own lives.

This book is a guide for anyone looking to achieve their definition of success. Whether you are a recent graduate starting your career, a seasoned professional seeking to takc your business to the next level, or simply someone looking to improve your personal life, the strategies and insights in this book will help you get there.

The chapters in this book are designed to take you on a ***journey of self-discovery and personal growth.*** Each chapter delves into a specific topic, from cultivating a success mindset and clarifying your vision to building habits, embracing failure, finding mentors, networking, leading with emotional intelligence, time management, and maintaining work-life balance.

Throughout this book, you will find quotes from renowned personalities who have achieved success in their respective fields. These quotes provide additional inspiration and wisdom, reminding us that success is not an overnight achievement, but rather a journey that requires hard work, perseverance, and a willingness to learn and grow.

As the author of this book, I have had the privilege of working with individuals from various backgrounds, including academicians, officials, entrepreneurs, executives, and individuals seeking personal growth. Through these experiences, I have learned that success is not just about setting and achieving goals, but it is also about cultivating the right mindset, building supportive habits and relationships, and maintaining a sense of balance in our lives.

In writing this book, I have drawn from my own experiences as well as the experiences of successful individuals I have worked with. I have also conducted extensive research on each topic, gathering insights from academic literature, industry experts, and personal anecdotes. This book is the culmination of years of learning and growth, and I hope it provides you with the tools and inspiration to achieve your own version of success.

It is my hope that this book will serve as a roadmap for your journey toward success, helping you to develop the mindset, habits, and relationships necessary to achieve your goals. I encourage you to approach this book with an open mind and a willingness to learn and apply the insights and strategies to your own life.

Remember, success is not a destination, but a journey. It is about continuous growth and development, and the willingness to learn from both successes and failures. I hope this book will help you on your journey toward achieving your definition of success and will guide all to achieve sustainable success.

Best regards,

Kailashi Punit D.
Writer

Acknowledgements

Writing a book is a journey, and I am grateful for the support and encouragement I have received along the way.

First and foremost, I want to thank my family for their unwavering support and belief in me. Your love and encouragement have been my rock throughout this journey.

I would also like to thank my mentors and coaches who have provided me with invaluable guidance and insights, and who have helped me develop the skills and mindset needed to achieve success.

To my colleagues and friends, thank you for your encouragement, and feedback, and for inspiring me with your own achievements.

I am also grateful to the many successful individuals who have shared their stories and insights with me, and who have provided me with the inspiration and motivation to pursue my own definition of success.

I would like to express my gratitude to the publisher and the entire team of ***KAILASHI GLOBAL PUBLICATIONS, INDIA*** who have been instrumental in bringing this book to life, and for their commitment to helping others achieve success.

Lastly, I want to thank the readers of this book, for your interest and willingness to learn and grow. It is my hope that the insights and strategies shared in this book will help you achieve your own version of success.

Thank you all for being a part of this journey with me.

Prologue

What does success mean to you?

Is it financial prosperity, career advancement, personal growth, or something else entirely?

"Success is not the absence of failure; it's the persistence through failure." - Aisha Tyler

For many of us, the definition of success is deeply personal and unique. It is a reflection of our values, aspirations, and dreams. Yet, regardless of our individual definitions of success, we all share a common desire to achieve it.

This book is a guide to help you achieve your own version of success. It is a collection of insights, strategies, and best practices from successful individuals who have achieved their goals and made their dreams a reality.

Throughout this book, you will learn **how to cultivate a success mindset, clarify your vision, build habits, overcome self-doubt, and leverage your network to achieve your goals.** You will also learn how to lead with emotional intelligence, manage your time and productivity, and maintain a healthy work-life balance.

But most importantly, this book is about **inspiring and empowering** you to take action towards achieving your goals. It is about showing you that success is within your reach and that with the right mindset, skills, and support, you can make your dreams a reality.

So, if you are ready to take the first step towards achieving your own version of success, I invite you to join me on this journey. Let's explore the insights and strategies that successful individuals have used to achieve their goals and make their dreams a reality. And let's work together to create a future filled with success, fulfillment, and happiness.

SUSTAINABLE SUCCESS

"Success is not just about achieving something. It's also about how you achieved it and the path you took to get there." - Swami Vivekananda

"Success is not about what you have, but about what you give back to society." - Mahatma Gandhi

Sustainable success is achieving success in a way that is not only financially profitable but also socially and environmentally responsible. It involves creating a business or career model that is resilient and can withstand changes in the economy, industry trends, and societal expectations.

Sustainable success is not just about short-term gains, but **about creating long-term value** for all stakeholders, including customers, employees, shareholders, and the environment. It involves making decisions that balance economic, social, and environmental considerations, rather than prioritizing one at the expense of others.

Sustainable success is about **creating a positive impact on the world** while achieving personal and professional goals. It requires a mindset shift from a focus solely on profit to a broader perspective that includes ethical considerations and the impact of one's actions on society and the environment. Ultimately, sustainable success is about leaving a positive legacy for future generations.

I

The Success Mindset: Cultivating a positive and resilient mindset for success

"Success is not a destination, it's a journey. The journey is what gives you happiness, not the destination." - A. P. J. Abdul Kalam, former President of India

"Success is not final, failure is not fatal: it is the courage to continue that counts." - Winston Churchill

The success mindset is an essential factor in achieving success in any area of life. It is a way of thinking that is focused on **growth, optimism, and resilience**, and it can help you overcome challenges and obstacles on the road to achieving your goals.

To cultivate a successful mindset, you need to **adopt a set of beliefs, attitudes, and habits** that support your goals and aspirations. These include-

@Embracing a Growth Mindset

The growth mindset is a belief that you can develop your skills, talents, and abilities through effort, practice, and learning. This mindset emphasizes the power of effort and persistence in achieving success, rather than innate talent or ability. When you have a growth mindset, you are more likely to take on challenges and view mistakes as opportunities to learn and grow, rather than setbacks or failures.

@Focusing on Solutions

A success mindset is focused on finding solutions to problems and challenges. Instead of dwelling on obstacles or setbacks, you look for ways to overcome them and move forward. This requires a positive attitude and a willingness to take risks and try new things.

@Being Resilient

Resilience is the ability to bounce back from setbacks and adversity. A success mindset requires resilience because you will inevitably face obstacles and challenges on the road to achieving your goals. When you are resilient, you are better able to stay motivated, maintain a positive attitude, and persevere through difficult times.

@Practicing Self-Compassion

Self-compassion is the ability to treat yourself with kindness and understanding, even when you make mistakes or face setbacks. A success mindset requires self-compassion because it can be easy to get discouraged or beat yourself up when things don't go as planned. When you practice self-compassion, you are more likely to bounce back from setbacks and maintain a positive attitude.

@Staying Positive

A success mindset requires a positive attitude and outlook. This means focusing on what is going well, even when things are challenging, and looking for opportunities and possibilities in any situation. When you maintain a positive attitude, you are better able to stay motivated and focused on your goals.

"Success is not the key to happiness. Happiness is the key to success. If you love what you are doing, you will be successful." - Albert Schweitzer

@Taking Action

A success mindset requires taking action toward your goals, even when you don't feel motivated or inspired. This means setting clear goals and taking intentional steps towards achieving them, even when it is difficult or uncomfortable. When you take action, you build momentum and create a sense of progress and accomplishment, which can fuel your motivation and keep you moving forward.

Cultivating a success mindset takes **time, effort, and practice,** but it is a skill that can be developed and strengthened over time.

Here are some strategies you can use to cultivate a success mindset:

@Set Clear Goals

Setting clear, specific, and achievable goals is an essential part of cultivating a success mindset. When you have a clear goal in mind, you can create a plan of action to achieve it, which can help you stay focused and motivated. Make sure your goals are measurable, time-bound, and aligned with your values and aspirations.

@Embrace a Growth Mindset

Adopting a growth mindset is another essential strategy for cultivating a success mindset. A growth mindset is a belief that you can improve your skills, knowledge, and abilities through effort, practice, and learning. When you have a growth mindset, you view challenges and failures as opportunities to learn and grow, rather than setbacks or failures. This mindset can help you stay motivated and persevere through difficult times.

@Practice Positive Self-Talk

The way you talk to yourself can have a significant impact on your mindset and motivation. When you practice positive self-talk, you replace negative, self-limiting thoughts with positive, empowering ones. For example, instead of telling yourself, "I'm not good enough," say, "I am capable of achieving my goals." Positive self-talk can help you build confidence, increase your motivation, and maintain a positive attitude.

@Focus on Solutions

A success mindset is focused on finding solutions to problems and challenges. Instead of dwelling on obstacles or setbacks, focus on what you can do to overcome them and move forward. This requires a positive attitude and a willingness to take risks and try new things. When you focus on solutions, you can stay motivated and make progress toward your goals.

@Practice Gratitude

Gratitude is the practice of focusing on what you have and appreciating the good things in your life. When you practice gratitude, you can shift your focus from what you lack to what you have, which can improve your mood and increase your sense of well-being. Gratitude can also help you stay motivated and focused on your goals, even when the road gets tough.

@Embrace Failure

Failure is an inevitable part of the journey to success. Instead of fearing failure, embrace it as an opportunity to learn and grow. When you experience failure, ask yourself what you can learn from the experience and how you can use that knowledge to improve. This mindset can help you stay motivated and persistent, even when you encounter obstacles and setbacks.

"The only limit to our realization of tomorrow will be our doubts of today." - Franklin D. Roosevelt

@Surround Yourself with Positive People

The people you surround yourself with can have a significant impact on your mindset and motivation. Surround yourself with positive, supportive people who believe in you and your goals. Avoid negative, critical people who bring you down or discourage you. When you surround yourself with positive people, you can stay motivated and inspired to achieve your goals.

Conclusion

These strategies can help you cultivate a success mindset and achieve your goals. Remember, cultivating a success mindset is a journey, not a destination. It takes time, effort, and practice, but with persistence and dedication, you can develop a success mindset that empowers you to achieve your dreams.

II

Clarifying Your Vision: Crafting a clear and compelling vision for your life and career

"The only way to do great work is to love what you do. If you haven't found it yet, keep looking. Don't settle. As with all matters of the heart, you'll know when you find it." - Steve Jobs

Having a clear and compelling vision for your life and career is essential for achieving your goals and fulfilling your potential. **A vision is a mental picture of the future you want to create for yourself.** It is a guiding principle that gives you direction and purpose in life. Without a clear vision, you may feel lost or stuck in your current situation, lacking direction and motivation.

Crafting a clear and compelling vision requires **clarity of purpose, self-awareness, and a deep understanding of what matters most to you.**

We will explore the steps you can take to clarify your vision and create a roadmap for achieving your goals.

@Reflect on Your Values and Priorities

The first step in clarifying your vision is to reflect on your values and priorities. Your values are the things that are most important to you, such as family, health, career, spirituality, or personal growth. Your priorities are the things you want to achieve or experiencc in life, such as financial stability, travel, education, or starting a business.

To clarify your vision, start by asking yourself what matters most to you. What are your core values? What are your top priorities in life? Write down your answers in a journal or a piece of paper.

@Create a Clear Picture of Your Future

"The best way to predict the future is to create it." - Peter Drucker

The next step is to create a clear picture of your future. Imagine yourself five, ten, or twenty years from now. What does your ideal life and career look like? What kind of work do you want to do? What kind of lifestyle do you want to have? Where do you want to live? Who do you want to spend time with?

As you imagine your future, try to be as specific and detailed as possible. Visualize yourself in your ideal career, doing work that you love and finding fulfillment in your job. See yourself living in your dream home, surrounded by people you love and doing the things you enjoy. Write down your vision in a journal or on a piece of paper.

@Identify Your Strengths and Passions

"The only thing worse than being blind is having sight but no vision." - Helen Keller

To achieve your vision, you need to leverage your strengths and passions. Your strengths are the skills, knowledge, and abilities that you excel at, while your passions are the things that you love to do and that bring you joy and fulfillment.

Take some time to identify your strengths and passions. What are you good at? What do you enjoy doing? How can you use your strengths and passions to achieve your vision? Write down your answers in a journal or on a piece of paper.

@Set Goals and Create an Action Plan

"You have to dream before your dreams can come true." - A. P. J. Abdul Kalam

The final step in clarifying your vision is to set goals and create an action plan. Your goals are the specific steps you need to take to achieve your vision. They should be specific, measurable, achievable, relevant, and time-bound.

To set your goals, break down your vision into smaller, achievable steps. What do you need to do to achieve your vision? What skills or knowledge do you need to acquire? What obstacles do you need to overcome? What resources do you need?

Once you have identified your goals, create an action plan to achieve them.

Break down your goals into specific tasks and set deadlines for each task. Create a schedule and a system for tracking your progress. Celebrate your successes along the way, and use setbacks as opportunities to learn and grow.

Conclusion

Clarifying your vision requires reflection, self-awareness, and goal-setting. By reflecting on your values and priorities, creating a clear picture of your future, identifying your strengths and passions, setting goals, and creating an action plan, you can create a roadmap for achieving your vision and living a fulfilling life. Remember that your vision may evolve over time, and it is okay to adjust your goals and action plan as needed.

III

Building Habits: Creating habits and routines that support your success

"We are what we repeatedly do. Excellence, then, is not an act, but a habit." - Aristotle"We are what we repeatedly do. Excellence, then, is not an act, but a habit." - Aristotle

Building habits is a crucial aspect of achieving success in any area of life. **Habits are the behaviors and actions that we repeat regularly, often unconsciously.** Developing positive habits and routines can help us stay focused, motivated, and productive while reducing stress and uncertainty.

We will explore the steps you can take to create habits and routines that support your success-

@Identify Your Goals and Priorities

The first step in building habits is to identify your goals and priorities. What do you want to achieve? What is most important to you? What are your long-term and short-term goals?

Once you have identified your goals and priorities, you can start to think about the habits and routines that will help you achieve them. For example, if your goal is to become more physically fit, you may need to develop a habit of exercising regularly or eating a healthy diet.

@Start Small

One of the keys to building habits is to start small. It can be tempting to try to make big changes all at once, but this often leads to frustration and failure. Instead, focus on developing small, manageable habits that you can stick to consistently.

For example, if you want to start a daily meditation practice, you may start by meditating for just five minutes each day, and gradually increase the time as you become more comfortable with the practice.

@Set Specific Goals and Deadlines

To create habits that stick, it's important to set specific goals and deadlines. Make your goals measurable and achievable, and set a deadline for achieving them. This will help you stay focused and motivated, and provide a clear sense of progress.

For example, if your goal is to read more books, you may set a goal of reading one book per month and set a deadline for finishing each book.

@Create a Routine

"The secret of change is to focus all of your energy, not on fighting the old, but on building the new." - Socrates

Building habits often requires creating a routine. A routine is a set of actions or behaviors that you perform regularly and consistently. By creating a routine, you can make your habits more automatic and easier to maintain.

For example, if your goal is to exercise more, you may create a routine of going to the gym at the same time each day or going for a run after work.

@Use Positive Reinforcement

Positive reinforcement is an essential aspect of building habits. When you reward yourself for positive behaviors, you create a positive association with those behaviors, making them more likely to become habits.

For example, if your goal is to save money, you may reward yourself each time you reach a savings milestone, such as saving Rs.1000 or paying off a credit card.

@Track Your Progress

Tracking your progress is an important part of building habits. It allows you to see how far you've come and identify areas where you need to improve. It also helps you stay motivated and focused on your goals.

There are many ways to track your progress, including using a journal, a habit-tracking app, or a calendar. Choose the method that works best for you and make it a regular part of your routine.

@Adjust and Adapt

Finally, it's important to remember that building habits are an ongoing process. Your goals, priorities, and circumstances may change over time, and your habits and routines may need to adapt accordingly.

Be willing to adjust your habits and routines as needed, and don't be too hard on yourself if you experience setbacks or challenges. Building habits is a journey, and it takes time, effort, and patience to create lasting change.

"The future depends on what you do today." - Mahatma Gandhi

Conclusion

Building habits and routines that support your success is essential for achieving your goals and living a fulfilling life. By identifying your goals and priorities, starting small, setting specific goals and deadlines, creating a routine, using positive reinforcement, tracking your progress

IV

Embracing Failure and Learning from Mistakes: How to turn setbacks and failures into Opportunities for growth

"I have not failed. I've just found 10,000 ways that won't work." - Thomas Edison

Embracing failure and learning from mistakes is an important aspect of achieving success. **Failure is an inevitable part of life,** and **setbacks are bound to happen on the path to achieving our goals.** However, it's how we respond to failure that determines our future success.

Now we will explore the steps you can take to embrace failure and learn from mistakes-

@Change Your Mindset

The first step in embracing failure is to change your mindset. Instead of seeing failure as something negative or shameful, try to reframe it as an opportunity for growth and learning.

Remember, some of the most successful people in history have experienced failure before achieving their goals. Walt Disney was fired from a job for lacking creativity, and Steve Jobs was ousted from his own company before later returning to lead it to success.

By changing your mindset and viewing failure as a natural part of the learning process, you can start to see setbacks as opportunities for growth and improvement.

@Analyze What Went Wrong

Once you've shifted your mindset, it's important to take a step back and analyze what went wrong. What led to the failure or setback? Were there specific actions or decisions that contributed to the outcome?

Be honest with yourself, but also be compassionate. Avoid blaming yourself or others, and focus on identifying the root causes of the problem.

@Learn from Your Mistakes

"Failure is simply the opportunity to begin again, this time more intelligently." - Henry Ford

After analyzing what went wrong, the next step is to learn from your mistakes. What lessons can you take away from the experience? What can you do differently next time?

By learning from your mistakes, you can avoid repeating the same errors in the future and improve your chances of success.

@Develop Resilience

Resilience is the ability to bounce back from setbacks and adversity. Developing resilience is an important part of embracing failure and learning from mistakes.

To develop resilience, it's important to cultivate a growth mindset, practice self-care, and build a support network of friends and family who can offer encouragement and guidance during difficult times.

@Take Action

Finally, it's important to take action after experiencing failure or setbacks. Use the lessons you've learned to make changes and improvements and continue to work towards your goals.

Remember, failure is not a final destination, but a temporary setback. By embracing failure and learning from mistakes, you can turn setbacks into opportunities for growth and ultimately achieve success.

Conclusion

Embracing failure and learning from mistakes is a critical part of achieving success. By changing your mindset, analyzing what went wrong, learning from your mistakes, developing resilience, and taking action, you can turn setbacks into opportunities for growth and improvement. Remember, success is not defined by the absence of failure, but by the ability to overcome it and keep moving forward.

V

Finding Mentors and Coaches: Building a support system to help you achieve your goals

"The greatest good you can do for another is not just share your riches, but to reveal to him his own." - Benjamin Disraeli

Finding mentors and coaches is an important part of building a support system that can help you achieve your goals. Whether you are looking **to improve your skills, advance your career, or pursue a personal passion, mentors and coaches can provide guidance, support, and**

accountability to help you reach your full potential.

The five steps you can take to find mentors and coaches and build a strong support system-

@Define Your Goals and Needs

Before you start looking for mentors and coaches, it's important to define your goals and needs. What are you hoping to achieve? What specific skills or areas do you need help with?

By identifying your goals and needs, you can narrow your search for potential mentors and coaches who can provide the guidance and support you need.

@Identify Potential Mentors and Coaches

Once you have a clear understanding of your goals and needs, the next step is to identify potential mentors and coaches.

Start by looking within your existing network. Do you have any friends, colleagues, or acquaintances who have experience or expertise in your area of interest? Are there any professional organizations or networking groups you can join to connect with others in your field?

You can also look for mentors and coaches online. Many experts offer coaching services or mentorship programs, and social media platforms like LinkedIn can be a great way to connect with potential mentors and coaches.

@Reach Out and Build Relationships

Once you have identified potential mentors and coaches, the next step is to reach out and build relationships. Start by introducing yourself and expressing your interest in their work or experience. Be clear about what you are looking for and how you hope they can help you.

Remember, building relationships takes time and effort. Be patient and respectful, and focus on building genuine connections with your potential mentors and coaches.

@Be Open to Feedback and Guidance

"If you're not making mistakes, then you're not doing anything. I'm positive that a doer makes mistakes." - John Wooden

When working with mentors and coaches, it's important to be open to feedback and guidance. Remember, the goal of mentorship and coaching is to help you grow and develop, so be willing to listen to constructive criticism and take action on the advice you receive.

It's also important, to be honest, and transparent with your mentors and coaches. If you are struggling with a particular issue or need additional support, don't be afraid to ask for help.

@Pay It Forward

Finally, once you have found mentors and coaches who have helped you achieve your goals, it's important to pay it forward by helping others.

Mentorship and coaching are two-way streets, and by sharing your own knowledge and experience with others, you can help others achieve success and build a strong community of support.

Conclusion

Finding mentors and coaches is an important part of building a support system that can help you achieve your goals. By defining your goals and needs, identifying potential mentors and coaches, building relationships, being open to feedback and guidance, and paying it forward, you can build a strong support system that will help you reach your full potential. Remember, **success is not achieved alone but with the help and support of others.**

VI

Overcoming Self-Doubt and Imposter Syndrome: Strategies for managing self-doubt and imposter syndrome

"You have been criticizing yourself for years, and it hasn't worked. Try approving of

yourself and see what happens." - Louise Hay

Self-doubt and imposter syndrome are common challenges that many people face, especially when pursuing new goals or facing unfamiliar situations. **Self-doubt can be defined as a lack of confidence in one's abilities or judgment, while imposter syndrome refers to a feeling of inadequacy or fraudulence despite evidence of one's competence.**

These feelings of self-doubt and imposter syndrome can **hold us back and prevent us from reaching our full potential.** However, there are strategies we can use to manage these feelings and overcome them. In this article, we will explore some of these strategies.

@Recognize and Acknowledge Your Feelings

The first step in overcoming self-doubt and imposter syndrome is to recognize and acknowledge your feelings. It's important to understand that these feelings are normal and that many successful people have experienced them at some point in their lives.

Once you have recognized and acknowledged your feelings, you can begin to take steps to manage them.

@Reframe Your Self-Talk

"The only way to get rid of the fear of doing something is to go out and do it." - Susan Jeffers

Self-talk is the inner dialogue we have with ourselves, and it can greatly influence our self-perception and confidence.

When we engage in negative self-talk, we reinforce our feelings of self-doubt and imposter syndrome.

To overcome self-doubt and imposter syndrome, it's important to reframe your self-talk. Instead of focusing on your perceived weaknesses or inadequacies, focus on your strengths and accomplishments. Challenge negative thoughts and replace them with positive affirmations.

@Practice Self-Compassion

Self-compassion is the practice of treating yourself with kindness, understanding, and acceptance. When we are kind to ourselves, we are more likely to feel confident and capable.

To practice self-compassion, try treating yourself as you would treat a friend. Be understanding of your mistakes and shortcomings, and offer yourself words of encouragement and support.

@Set Realistic Goals

Setting realistic goals can help you build confidence and overcome self-doubt and imposter syndrome. When you set achievable goals and work towards them, you gain a sense of accomplishment and progress.

However, it's important to set goals that are challenging but realistic. Setting goals that are too difficult or unrealistic can reinforce feelings of self-doubt and imposter syndrome.

@Celebrate Your Successes

Celebrating your successes can help you build confidence and overcome self-doubt and imposter syndrome. When you acknowledge your achievements, you reinforce the belief in your abilities and competence.

Take time to celebrate your successes, no matter how small they may be. Celebrate your progress and the milestones you have achieved.

@Seek Support

Seeking support from others can be an effective way to manage self-doubt and imposter syndrome. Talk to friends, family, or colleagues about your feelings and experiences. Join a support group or seek the guidance of a therapist or coach.

By seeking support, you can gain perspective and insight, and develop strategies to manage your feelings of self-doubt and imposter syndrome.

"Self-doubt kills more dreams than failure ever will." - Suzy Kassem, author and poet

Conclusion

Self-doubt and imposter syndrome **are common challenges** that many people face. However, by recognizing and acknowledging your feelings, reframing your self-talk, practicing self-compassion, setting realistic goals, celebrating your successes, and seeking support, you can manage these feelings and overcome them. Remember, self-doubt and imposter syndrome do not define your abilities or worth. You are capable and deserving of success.

VII

The Power of Networking: Building relationships and leveraging your network for success

"If you want to go fast, go alone. If you want to go far, go together." - African Proverb

Networking is an essential aspect of building a successful career or business. It involves building relationships with people in your industry or field, exchanging information, and leveraging those connections to achieve your goals.

Let's explore the power of networking and how you can use it to build your own success-

@Expand Your Network

The first step in leveraging the power of networking is to expand your network. Attend industry events, conferences, and networking events. Join professional organizations and social media groups related to your field.

Networking is not just about meeting new people; it's about building and maintaining relationships. Take the time to get to know the people you meet, and follow up with them after the event.

@Build Authentic Relationships

Networking is not just about exchanging business cards or promoting yourself. It's about building authentic relationships based on trust, mutual interests, and shared values.

Take the time to get to know the people you meet. Ask them about their interests, goals, and challenges. Show a genuine interest in their work and accomplishments.

@Offer Value

Networking is a two-way street. It's not just about what you can get from others, but also about what you can offer them. Offer your skills, expertise, and resources to help others achieve their goals.

By offering value, you build a reputation as a helpful and reliable person, which can lead to new opportunities and collaborations.

@Follow Up

Following up is an important part of building relationships and leveraging your network. After you meet someone, send them a follow-up email or message. Keep in touch with them on social media, and share their content or achievements.

Following up shows that you value the relationship and are interested in maintaining it. It can also lead to new opportunities and collaborations.

@Be Authentic

Authenticity is key in building strong relationships and leveraging your network. Be true to yourself and your values, and don't try to be someone you're not.

When you are authentic, people are more likely to trust and respect you. They are also more likely to refer you to others and help you achieve your goals.

@Leverage Your Network

"Your success in life is directly proportional to the number of people you serve and how well you serve them." - Zig Ziglar

Once you have built a strong network, it's important to leverage it to achieve your goals. Reach out to your connections for advice, referrals, or collaborations.

When you ask for help, be specific about what you need and how your connection can help. Offer value in return, and show appreciation for their help.

@Give Back

Networking is not just about what you can get from others; it's also about what you can give back. Help others in your network achieves their goals, and offer your expertise and resources when needed.

Giving back strengthens your relationships and builds goodwill. It also increases the likelihood that others will help you when you need it.

Conclusion

Networking is a powerful tool for building a successful career or business. By expanding your network, building authentic relationships, offering value, following up, being authentic, leveraging your network, and giving back, you can build a strong network and leverage it to achieve your goals. Remember, networking is not just about what you can get from others; it's also about what you can offer them. By building strong relationships based on trust and mutual interests, you can create a network that supports and enhances your success.

VIII

Leading with Emotional Intelligence: Developing emotional intelligence skills for effective leadership

"The greatest leader is not necessarily the one who does the greatest things. He is the one

that gets the people to do the greatest things."
- Ronald Reagan

Effective leadership requires more than just technical skills and knowledge. It also requires emotional intelligence, the ability to understand and manage one's own emotions, as well as those of others.

We will now explore the importance of emotional intelligence in leadership and how to develop these skills-

@What is Emotional Intelligence?

Emotional intelligence is the ability to understand and manage one's own emotions, as well as those of others. It involves the ability to perceive, express, understand, and regulate emotions.

Emotional intelligence is essential in leadership because it allows leaders to understand and connect with their team members on a deeper level, leading to better communication, collaboration, and productivity.

@Develop Self-Awareness

Self-awareness is the first step in developing emotional intelligence. It involves understanding one's own emotions, strengths, and weaknesses.

Leaders should take the time to reflect on their emotions, and how they affect their behavior and decision-making. They should also seek feedback from others to gain a better understanding of how they are perceived.

@Practice Self-Regulation

Self-regulation is the ability to manage one's own emotions, thoughts, and behaviors. It involves staying calm and composed in stressful situations, and avoiding impulsive or reactive behaviors.

Leaders should practice self-regulation by taking a step back and assessing the situation before reacting. They should also practice techniques such as deep breathing or meditation to help them stay calm in high-pressure situations.

@Develop Empathy

Empathy is the ability to understand and share the feelings of others. It involves putting oneself in another person's shoes and seeing things from their perspective.

Leaders should develop empathy by actively listening to their team members and seeking to understand their perspective. They should also be aware of nonverbal cues and other signals that indicate how a person is feeling.

@Build Relationships

"Leadership is not about being in charge. It's about taking care of those in your charge." - Simon Sinek

Building relationships is essential in leadership, and emotional intelligence plays a critical role in this process. Leaders should take the time to connect with their team members on a personal level, and seek to build trust and respect.

Leaders can build relationships by showing an interest in their team members‘ lives and hobbies, and by celebrating their achievements and successes. They should also be transparent and honest in their communication, and be open to feedback and criticism.

@Communicate Effectively

Effective communication is essential in leadership, and emotional intelligence can help leaders communicate more effectively. Leaders should be aware of their tone and body language, and ensure that their message is clear and concise.

Leaders should also be good listeners, and seek to understand their team members' perspective. They should encourage open communication and create a safe and supportive environment where team members feel comfortable expressing their thoughts and ideas.

@Manage Conflict

Conflict is inevitable in any workplace, but emotional intelligence can help leaders manage conflict more effectively. Leaders should be aware of their own emotions and biases, and seek to understand the perspectives of all parties involved.

Leaders should also practice active listening and seek to find common ground and a win-win solution. They should be open to compromise, and be willing to apologize and make amends if necessary.

Conclusion

Emotional intelligence is essential for effective leadership. Developing self-awareness, self-regulation, empathy, building relationships, effective communication, and conflict management skills can help leaders connect with their team members on a deeper level and create a more productive and positive work environment. By practicing these skills, leaders can inspire their team members, build trust and respect, and achieve their goals.

IX

Time Management and Productivity: Maximizing your time and productivity to achieve your goals

"The key is not to prioritize what's on your schedule, but to schedule your priorities." - Stephen Covey

Time management and productivity are critical factors in achieving one's goals. In today's **fast-paced world, it's easy to become overwhelmed with work and personal**

responsibilities, leading to stress and burnout.

We will discuss some effective strategies for managing time and increasing productivity-

@Identify Your Priorities

The first step in effective time management is identifying your priorities. You need to determine what tasks are most important and require your immediate attention. This will help you avoid wasting time on tasks that are not essential and allow you to focus on what's important.

@Create a Schedule

"The bad news is time flies. The good news is you're the pilot." - Michael Altshuler, motivational speaker

Creating a schedule is an effective way to manage your time and increase productivity. It involves planning out your day or week, scheduling specific times for each task, and sticking to the plan.

Start by creating a to-do list for the day or week, then prioritize each task according to importance. Schedule specific times for each task, ensuring that you have enough time to complete each one. Use a calendar or scheduling app to keep track of your schedule and make adjustments as necessary.

@Avoid Procrastination

Procrastination is one of the biggest barriers to productivity. It's easy to put off tasks that are difficult or unpleasant, but this only leads to more stress and a bigger workload.

To avoid procrastination, break down large tasks into smaller, more manageable ones. Set deadlines for each task and hold yourself accountable for completing them. Eliminate distractions by turning off your phone or email notifications and focusing solely on the task at hand.

@Delegate Tasks

Delegating tasks is an effective way to increase productivity and manage time more efficiently. Identify tasks that can be delegated to others, such as administrative or routine tasks, and assign them to team members who have the necessary skills and expertise.

This frees up your time to focus on more important tasks that require your immediate attention. It also helps to build trust and empower your team members, leading to increased job satisfaction and productivity.

@Use Time-Blocking

Time-blocking is a technique that involves scheduling specific times for each task, similar to creating a schedule. However, it goes a step further by allocating specific blocks of time for each task, ensuring that you have enough time to complete each one.

To use time-blocking, divide your day into specific time blocks and allocate tasks to each block. For example, you may allocate 30 minutes for responding to emails, 2 hours for completing a project, and 1 hour for a meeting. Stick to the schedule as closely as possible, adjusting it as necessary.

@Take Breaks

Taking breaks is essential for maintaining productivity and avoiding burnout. It allows your mind and body to rest and recharge, leading to increased energy and focus.

Schedule regular breaks throughout the day, such as a 10-minute walk or a coffee break. Use this time to clear your mind and refocus on the task at hand. It's also important to take longer breaks, such as a vacation or a weekend away, to completely disconnect from work and recharge.

@Use Technology to Your Advantage

Technology can be a valuable tool for managing time and increasing productivity. Use scheduling apps, project management tools, and time-tracking apps to keep track of your schedule and tasks.

Automate routine tasks such as email responses and social media posts using tools such as Hootsuite or Buffer. Use productivity tools such as RescueTime to track how you're spending your time and identify areas for improvement.

Conclusion

Effective time management and productivity are essential for achieving your goals. By identifying priorities, creating a schedule, avoiding procrastination, delegating tasks, using time-blocking, taking breaks, and using technology to your advantage, you can maximize your time and increase productivity. These strategies not only help to reduce stress and avoid burnout but also lead to increased job satisfaction

X

Maintaining Work-Life Balance: Balancing your personal and professional life to avoid burnout and increase happiness

"Happiness is not a matter of intensity but of balance, order, rhythm and harmony." - Thomas Merton

Maintaining work-life balance is crucial for both our personal and professional well-being. With the fast-paced world we live in, it's easy to lose track of time and prioritize work over personal life. However, it's important to understand that **our personal lives are just as important as our professional** lives, and neglecting one for the other can lead to burnout, stress, and even health problems.

Strategies for maintaining work-life balance-

@Set Boundaries

One of the most important steps in maintaining work-life balance is setting boundaries. This means deciding on the time you want to allocate to work and personal life and sticking to it. This can be challenging, especially if you work from home, but it's essential to create a clear separation between work and personal life. Set specific working hours and try to stick to them as much as possible. When your workday is over, avoid checking work emails or taking work-related calls.

@Prioritize Self-Care

Self-care is essential for maintaining work-life balance. When we neglect our physical and emotional well-being, it's easy to become overwhelmed and burnt out. Make time for exercise, healthy eating, and getting enough sleep. It's also important to take time for yourself to do things that you enjoy, such as hobbies, reading, or spending time with friends and family.

@Use Technology to Your Advantage

Technology has made our lives easier in many ways, but it can also be a source of distraction and stress. To maintain work-life balance, use technology to your advantage. Use productivity apps to manage your time and keep track of your tasks. Set notifications and alerts to remind you of important deadlines or appointments. But be mindful of the time you spend on social media or other non-work related apps.

@Learn to Say No

Saying no can be challenging, especially when it comes to work-related requests. However, it's essential to learn to say no when it's necessary. If you're already overloaded with work or personal commitments, saying yes to new requests can lead to overwhelm and stress. Be honest about your limitations and communicate them clearly to your colleagues or friends and family.

@Create a Supportive Environment

Surround yourself with people who support your work-life balance goals. This includes your colleagues, friends, and family. Communicate your needs clearly and ask for support when necessary. If you have children, consider hiring a babysitter or getting help from a family member to help you with child care. A supportive environment can go a long way in maintaining work-life balance.

@Take Breaks

Taking breaks throughout the workday is essential for maintaining productivity and avoiding burnout. Take short breaks every few hours to stretch, take a walk or simply take some time to relax. It's also important to take regular vacations to recharge and take time for yourself.

@Evaluate Your Priorities

"The challenge of work-life balance is without question one of the most significant struggles faced by modern man." - Stephen Covey

Evaluate your priorities regularly to ensure you're spending your time and energy on things that matter most to you. Make a list of your personal and professional goals and evaluate them regularly to ensure you're making progress towards achieving them. This can help you make informed decisions about how to spend your time and energy.

Conclusion

Maintaining work-life balance is essential for our **physical and emotional well-being.** By setting boundaries, prioritizing self-care, using technology to your advantage, learning to say no, creating a supportive environment, taking breaks, and evaluating your priorities regularly, you can achieve work-life balance and avoid burnout. Remember, work is important, but so is your personal life, so it's crucial to find a healthy balance between the two.

XI

How to Achieve Sustainable Success: Corporates

Achieving sustainable success is a complex and multifaceted endeavor that requires a deep understanding of **the interconnectedness of social, economic, and environmental factors.** It involves creating a career model that is resilient and can withstand changes in the economy, industry trends, and societal expectations. Here are some strategies that can help individuals and organizations achieve sustainable success:

@Re-Define Success

Before embarking on a journey toward sustainable success, it is important to define what success means to you or your organization. This can involve identifying your core values, setting achievable goals, and establishing metrics to track progress.

@Practice Ethical Leadership

Sustainable success requires leaders who prioritize ethics, integrity, and social responsibility. Leaders should act as role models by practicing ethical decision-making and encouraging their teams to do the same.

@Build a Culture of Sustainability

A culture of sustainability involves creating a workplace environment that encourages responsible practices and fosters a sense of environmental and social responsibility. This can involve establishing sustainable policies and practices, encouraging employee engagement, and promoting sustainable behaviors.

@Incorporate Sustainability into Your Products and Services

Sustainable success involves creating products and services that are environmentally and socially responsible. This can involve using eco-friendly materials, reducing waste, and supporting fair trade practices.

@Implement Sustainable Supply Chain Practices

Supply chain management is an essential component of achieving sustainable success. This involves sourcing materials and services from suppliers that adhere to sustainable practices, reducing waste, and implementing efficient logistics and distribution processes.

@Embrace Innovation

Innovation is key to achieving sustainable success. This can involve developing new technologies, products, and services that are environmentally and socially responsible, as well as exploring new business models that prioritize sustainability.

@Measure and Track Progress

Sustainable success requires ongoing monitoring and evaluation of progress. This involves setting and tracking metrics, reporting on environmental and social impact, and making adjustments as needed.

@Engage Stakeholders

Engaging stakeholders, including customers, employees, investors, and the wider community, is essential to achieving sustainable success. This involves listening to feedback, responding to concerns, and building relationships based on mutual respect and trust.

@Collaborate With Others

Collaboration is key to achieving sustainable success. This involves partnering with other organizations, industry groups, and government agencies to address shared challenges and develop sustainable solutions.

@Continuously Learn and Improve

Sustainable success requires a continuous learning and improvement mindset. This involves seeking out new knowledge and expertise, staying up-to-date on emerging trends and best practices, and using this knowledge to inform decision-making and drive innovation.

Achieving sustainable success is a long-term journey that requires **commitment, dedication, and a willingness to learn and adapt.** By incorporating these strategies into their daily practices, individuals and organizations can create a more sustainable future for themselves and their communities.

XII

How to Achieve Sustainable Success: Individuals

Sustainable success is about achieving long-term and meaningful results while maintaining a healthy balance between various aspects of our lives. In other words, it is about achieving **success that lasts and enhances our overall well-being.** Individual sustainable success can be achieved by **adopting certainhabits, values, and attitudes that promote personal growth and resilience**. In this article, we will discuss some key strategies for achieving sustainable success as an individual.

@Develop a success mindset

The first step towards achieving sustainable success is to develop a success mindset. This means cultivating a positive and resilient attitude towards challenges and setbacks. Success mindset involves believing in oneself and one's abilities, having a growth mindset, and embracing failures as opportunities to learn and grow. A success mindset can be developed through reading books, attending seminars, practicing positive self-talk, and surrounding oneself with positive and supportive people.

@Set clear goals

The second step towards achieving sustainable success is to set clear goals. This means defining what you want to achieve and creating a roadmap to get there. Clear goals help you to focus your efforts, track your progress, and stay motivated. It is important to set SMART goals, which are Specific, Measurable, Attainable, Relevant, and Time-bound. SMART goals provide clarity and direction and make it easier to break down big goals into smaller, achievable tasks.

@Build positive habits

The third step towards achieving sustainable success is to build positive habits. Habits are powerful because they shape our behavior and ultimately determine our outcomes. Positive habits are those that support our goals and values and promote our well-being. Examples of positive habits include regular exercise, healthy eating, meditation, reading, and journaling. Building positive habits takes time and effort but can have a significant impact on our success and happiness.

@Cultivate emotional intelligence

The fourth step towards achieving sustainable success is to cultivate emotional intelligence. Emotional intelligence is the ability to understand and manage our own emotions and those of others. It involves skills such as self-awareness, self-regulation, empathy, and social skills. Cultivating emotional intelligence can help us to navigate complex social situations, manage conflicts, and build positive relationships. Emotional intelligence can be developed through mindfulness practices, self-reflection, and seeking feedback from others.

@Seek continuous learning and improvement

The fifth step towards achieving sustainable success is to seek continuous learning and improvement. This means developing a growth mindset and a curiosity for learning new things. Continuous learning helps us to stay relevant, adapt to change, and expand our horizons. It can involve reading books, attending seminars, taking courses, or seeking mentorship. Continuous learning also requires a willingness to embrace feedback and learn from failures.

@Maintain work-life balance

The sixth step towards achieving sustainable success is to maintain work-life balance. This means balancing the demands of work with the needs of personal life such as family, friends, and hobbies. Maintaining work-life balance helps to prevent burnout, reduce stress, and increase overall well-being. It involves setting boundaries, prioritizing self-care, and making time for activities that bring joy and relaxation.

@Build a support system

The seventh step towards achieving sustainable success is to build a support system. This means surrounding oneself with positive and supportive people who can offer guidance, feedback, and encouragement. A support system can include family, friends, mentors, coaches, or colleagues. Building a support system requires being open and vulnerable, seeking help when needed, and offering support to others.

Conclusion

Achieving sustainable success as an individual requires a combination of mindset, goals, habits, emotional intelligence, continuous learning, work-life balance, and a support system. By adopting these strategies and making them a part of our daily lives, we can achieve long-term success and well-being. Remember that success is not a destination but a journey.

About The Author

Kailashi Punit D. is a multi-talented writer, poet, economist, motivational writer, and speaker. Born and raised in India, Kailashi developed a passion for writing at a young age and began crafting poetry and short stories.

After completing her studies in economics, Kailashi started his career as an assistant professor in economics and later on as an administrative statistician and economist, but never lost his love for writing. Over time, he began to explore the field of motivational writing and speaking, drawing on his personal experiences and knowledge of economics to inspire others to achieve their goals and live a successful life.

Kailashi has written several books on motivation, life, success, and personal development, including "The Road to Success," which has become a popular guide for individuals seeking to reach their full potential. His work is known for its practical, actionable advice, and its ability to inspire readers to take action toward their goals.

In addition to his writing, Kailashi is also a sought-after speaker, delivering motivational talks and workshops on a variety of topics, including leadership, personal development, and entrepreneurship. He has spoken at conferences, universities, and corporate events, inspiring audiences with his insights and wisdom.

Kailashi's writing and speaking have earned him a devoted following around the world, and she continues to inspire and motivate others to achieve their dreams and live successful lives.

SUMMARY

"The Road to Sustainable Success" is a comprehensive guide for anyone who wants to achieve their goals and live a successful life. The book covers a wide range of topics, from cultivating a success mindset to building habits, clarifying your vision, embracing failure, finding mentors and coaches, leading with emotional intelligence, networking, time management, and maintaining work-life balance.

The book emphasizes the importance of developing a success mindset, which involves cultivating a positive and resilient attitude towards challenges and setbacks, setting clear goals, and taking consistent action toward achieving those goals. The author provides practical strategies and exercises for readers to develop their success mindsets, such as practicing gratitude, visualization, and self-reflection.

The book also emphasizes the importance of building habits and routines that support your success, such as creating a morning routine, prioritizing your most important tasks, and avoiding distractions. The author provides tips and techniques for readers to build these habits and make them stick.

Another key theme of the book is the importance of embracing failure and learning from mistakes. The author provides guidance on how to reframe failures as opportunities for growth and development, and how to use setbacks as a springboard for future success.

The book also emphasizes the importance of building a support system, including finding mentors and coaches, networking, and leading with emotional intelligence. The author provides practical strategies for readers to build these relationships and leverage their network for success.

Finally, the book provides guidance on time management and productivity, including strategies for maximizing your time and achieving your goals, and maintaining work-life balance, including self-care and mindfulness practices.

Overall, "The Road to Sustainable Success" is a practical and inspirational guide for anyone who wants to achieve their goals and live a successful life.

Important Points Covered

Building Habits
- Clarifying Your Vision
- Embracing Failure and Learning from Mistakes
- Finding Mentors and Coaches
- Goal Setting
- Imposter Syndrome
- Leadership
- Maintaining Work-Life Balance
- Mindfulness
- Networking
- Overcoming Self-Doubt
- Productivity
- Resilience
- Self-Care
- Success Mindset
- Sustainable Success
- Time Management

REFERENCES

Covey, S. R. (2004). The 7 Habits of Highly Effective People. Free Press.

Dweck, C. S. (2006). Mindset: The New Psychology of Success. Ballantine Books.

Duckworth, A. (2016). Grit: The Power of Passion and Perseverance. Scribner.

Gladwell, M. (2008). Outliers: The Story of Success. Little, Brown and Company.

Grant, A. M. (2013). Give and Take: A Revolutionary Approach to Success. Viking.

Heath, C., & Heath, D. (2010). Switch: How to Change Things When Change Is Hard. Crown Business.

Pink, D. H. (2011). Drive: The Surprising Truth About What Motivates Us. Riverhead Books.

Roth, G. (2015). The Achievement Habit: Stop Wishing, Start Doing, and Take Command of Your Life. Harper Business.

Sinek, S. (2011). Start with Why: How Great Leaders Inspire Everyone to Take Action. Portfolio.

Covey, S. R. (1991). Principle-centered leadership. Free Press.

Csikszentmihalyi, M. (1990). Flow: The Psychology of Optimal Experience. Harper & Row.

Duhigg, C. (2012). The Power of Habit: Why We Do What We Do in Life and Business. Random House.

Ferriss, T. (2007). The 4-Hour Work Week: Escape 9-5, Live Anywhere, and Join the New Rich. Crown.

Gladwell, M. (2013). David and Goliath: Underdogs, Misfits, and the Art of Battling Giants. Little, Brown and Company.

Godin, S. (2007). The Dip: A Little Book That Teaches You When to Quit (and When to Stick). Portfolio.

Johnson, S. (2010). Where Good Ideas Come From: The Natural History of Innovation. Riverhead Books.

Kahneman, D. (2011). Thinking, Fast and Slow. Farrar, Straus and Giroux.

Kiyosaki, R. T. (2000). Rich Dad, Poor Dad: What the Rich Teach Their Kids About Money That the Poor and Middle Class Do Not!. Warner Books.

Maxwell, J. C. (2011). The 21 Irrefutable Laws of Leadership: Follow Them and People Will Follow You. HarperCollins.

Ziglar, Z. (2012). See You at the Top. Pelican Publishing.

FURTHER

Disclaimer

The information provided in the book is for educational and informational purposes only and the author and publisher are not liable for any damages or consequences resulting from the use of this information.

Printed by Libri Plureos GmbH in Hamburg,
Germany